THE UAE — VISIONS OF CHANGE

THE UAE
VISIONS OF CHANGE

Through the lens of Noor Ali Rashid

MOTIVATE
PUBLISHING

Published by Motivate Publishing
Dubai: PO Box 2331, Dubai, UAE
Tel: (04) 2824060, Fax: (04) 2824436
Abu Dhabi: PO Box 43072, Abu Dhabi, UAE
Tel: (02) 271666, Fax: (02) 271888
London: Stewart's Court, 220 Stewart's Road, London SW8 4UD.
Tel: (44) 0207 627 2481, Fax: (44) 0207 720 3158

Directors: Obaid Humaid Al Tayer, Ian Fairservice
Editors: Ian Fairservice, Catherine Demangeot, Kate John
Editorial Consultants: Bob Milne Home, Peter Hellyer

First published 1997
Reprinted 1999

ISBN: 1 86063 017 0

British Library Cataloguing-in-Publication Data.
A catalogue record for this book is
available from the British Library.

Printed by Emirates Printing Press, Dubai.

While every care has been taken to identify
the people and places featured in the photographs
of this book it is possible that readers may be able to
provide further information. The publisher would
be happy to consider such additional details
for inclusion in future editions.

CONTENTS

THE UAE – VISIONS OF CHANGE represents many years of Noor Ali Rashid's prodigious work. Noor Ali has enjoyed a close relationship with the leaders of the United Arab Emirates, and therefore has had a unique position from which to witness and record many momentous events in our recent history.

VISIONS OF CHANGE tells an exciting story. It is a story of national accomplishments and progress told through photographs taken by a talented photographer. The pictures offer a rich and unparalleled view of some of the historical events in our country and the result is a valuable source of historical information.

From this pictorial account emerges a sense, not only of our national achievements, but also of the character of our leaders. We come to appreciate the role played by His Highness the President, Sheikh Zayed bin Sultan Al Nahyan, in the formation and development of the state. The major contributions of His Highness Sheikh Rashid bin Saeed Al Maktoum, as well as the Rulers of the other Emirates, are also well documented. In addition, the book captures the evolving and changing life in the United Arab Emirates over the last 40 years.

The old saying that 'a picture is worth a thousand words' is well demonstrated in this book. Captions to the pictures provide an introduction, but the photographs themselves complete the story in a fashion that words alone can not achieve. Noor Ali has been unusually successful in the wide range of pictorial material through which he demonstrates important moments of our recent history. As we have come to expect from Noor Ali, there are many surprises in this book for those who pause to look, read, and enjoy this delightful insight to our past.

I am confident that this book will be a worthy contribution to the ongoing effort to document and highlight the fascinating heritage of our country. I am also confident that this book, like Noor Ali's first two books on Abu Dhabi and Dubai respectively, will be well received by interested readers everywhere.

Nahyan bin Mubarak Al Nahyan
*Minister of Higher Education and
Scientific Research,
United Arab Emirates*

HISTORY IN THE MAKING

The United Arab Emirates is now widely acknowledged to be one of the most modern countries in the world in terms of its infrastructure, its buildings and its health and education systems. Yet, little more than three decades ago, the country had barely begun its process of development. In many areas, particularly away from the main coastal towns, life had scarcely changed in centuries.

The process of the country's economic and social development, compressing centuries into a mere few years, is a story that can be told in words that reflect dry and dusty statistics, of the growth in the numbers of schools and students, of the number of kilometres of paved roads or of the changes in building styles from simple one-storey houses to massive state-of-the-art skyscrapers.

Alternatively, it can be told largely in pictures, reflecting the changes in images that are, for the most part, much more memorable than a recitation of words and achievements.

In this book, the story of that change is told through the lens of Noor Ali Rashid, who took his first pictures in the Emirates, then the Trucial States, around 40 years ago, just as the first signs of development were beginning to appear. The earliest pictures show some of what the country used to be like, and if those pictures are accompanied by commentary that refers back to the 19th century and beyond, that, in itself, is a reflection of how little the country had changed in the period since.

From then onwards, however, the process gathers pace, and, likewise, so do the pictures reflect the acceleration of change.

The 'Visions of Change' in this book do not pretend to record everything, nor do they follow in strict chronological order, for such is not the way of a photographer. Instead, they illustrate the process of change and development by themes. Such themes include the emergence of the federation and the government structure; the process of the building of the infrastructure; the way in which the country began to make its impact upon the rest of the world, receiving political leaders from throughout the globe. Not many years before, few would have been aware of the precise location of the Emirates. Another theme, one of great importance in the Emirates today, is that of the traditional culture and heritage of the people, which, drawing upon roots that are hundreds of years old, have succeeded in surviving, indeed thriving, amidst the remarkable changes that have revolutionised society in the Emirates.

Noor Ali Rashid has had an ideal vantage point from which to record the process of the changing Emirates. A close companion of members of the ruling families of the country for over 40 years, he has been able, not only to record the changes that have taken place as if seen through their eyes, but also been able to picture those ruling family members themselves over the years too, thus providing a unique record of the emergence of the United Arab Emirates today.

That record represents an archive of enormous importance for the modern history of the country, one which will continue to be mined in the years ahead by researchers studying the evolution of the Emirates. It represents too, of course, something of great value for the people of the Emirates themselves. As the process of development got under way, there were few photographers around to record the scene, and of those, none had more privileged access on a long-term basis than Noor Ali Rashid. For the older generation, it records a life they can recall and remember, but of which they have previously had no pictorial record.

At the same time, however, his archive, from which a limited selection of pictures has been drawn to provide this pictorial record of *VISIONS OF CHANGE*, is an asset of great importance as a way of educating the younger generation of citizens of the Emirates and expatriate visitors and residents, providing them with a visual way of understanding the dramatic progress that has occurred within little more than a single generation.

THE FAIRMONT DUBAI MEETING FACILITIES

Floor plan 33rd storey

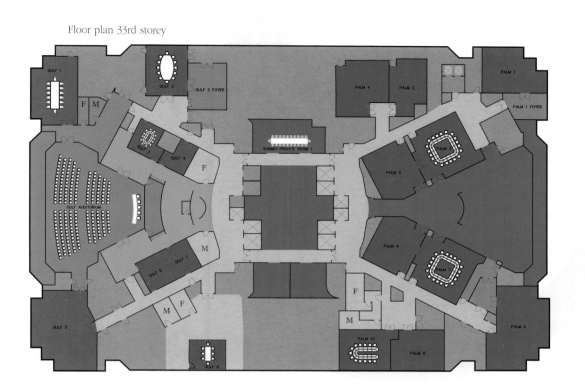

Key

▨	Auditorium
▨	Pre Function Area
▨	Meeting Rooms
▨	Pre Function Area
▨	Reception/Lounge Areas
F	Female Washroom
M	Male Washroom
⊠	Elevators
▨	Service Area

N

Location and name	Fixed Furniture	Sq. Metres	Ceiling Heights	Sq. Feet	Ceiling Heights	Classroom	Theatre	Boardroom	Hollow Square	Open U	Stand Up	Seated Meal Functions
BALLROOM - 1st Floor*												
Barajeel Ballroom		792	6.90	8525	22.6	500	850				895	600
Barajeel Ballroom A		255	6.90	2745	22.6	150	250		60	45	288	190
Barajeel Ballroom B		266	6.90	2863	22.6	160	260		60	45	301	190
Barajeel Ballroom C		255	6.90	2745	22.6	150	250		60	45	288	190
Barajeel Ballroom Prefunction		351	4.00	3781	13.1							
Barajeel Ballroom Upper Foyer		265	2.50	2855	8.2						80	
Barajeel Ballroom Lounge		35		377								
33rd EXECUTIVE CONFERENCE CENTRE - 33rd Floor												
Auditorium	Seminar Seating	154	2.7	1658	8.9	154						
Gulf 1	Boardroom	77	2.7	829	8.9			16				
Gulf 2	Boardroom	25	2.7	269	8.9			12				
Gulf 2 Foyer	Lounge Seating										20	
Gulf 3	Boardroom	25	2.4	265	7.9			10				
Gulf 4	Prayer Room	18	2.4	189	7.9							
Gulf 5		68	2.7	1000	8.9	42	90	30	24	30	110	70
Gulf 6		23	2.4	248	7.9							
Gulf 7		21	2.4	227	7.9							
Gulf 8												
Summit	Dinner Service	134	9.7	1442	31.8							80
Summit Private Room 1	Boardroom Dining	58	9.7	624	31.8			22				
Summit Private Room 2	Boardroom Dining	30	2.7	323	8.9			10				
Summit Private Room 3	Boardroom Dining	30	2.7	323	8.9			10				
Fairmont Gold Lounge		230	3.0	2475	9.8							
Palm 1		68	2.4	732	7.9	27	40				60	40
Palm 1 Foyer												
Palm 2	Boardroom	46	2.4	495	7.9	21	35					
Palm 3	Hollow Square	62	2.4	667	7.9				20			
Palm 4		64	2.4	689	7.9	21	40				50	32
Palm 5		63	2.4	673	7.9	27	36	20	16	15	50	40
Palm 6		112	2.4	1205	7.9	48	100	30	24	30	110	70
Palm 7	Boardroom	46	2.4	495	7.9			20				
Palm 8		51	2.4	549	7.9	27	40	20	16	15	45	32
Palm 9		63	2.4	678	7.9	27	36	20	16	15	50	32
Palm 10	Executive U	50	2.4	538	7.9					14		
THE EXCHANGE BUSINESS FLOOR - 2nd Floor*												
The Exchange Executive Boardroom	Boardroom	44	2.7	474	8.9			12				
The Exchange Boardroom A	Round	56	2.8	603	9.2			14				
The Exchange Boardroom B	Boardroom	43	2.8	463	9.2			12				
The Exchange Business Lounge	Lounge Seating											
The Exchange Dining Room 1	Boardroom Dining	19	2.8	208	9.2							10
The Exchange Dining Room 2	Boardroom Dining	24	2.8	256	9.2							8
The Exchange Dining Room 3	Boardroom Dining	25	2.8	264	9.2							10
SPECTRUM on ONE -1st Floor*												
Spectrum on One	Dinner Service											250
Spectrum on One Private Room 1	Boardroom Dining											12
Spectrum on One Private Room 2	Boardroom Dining											10
Spectrum on One Private Room 3	Boardroom Dining											8
Spectrum on One Private Room 4	Boardroom Dining											6

* Floor plans available upon request

THE Fairmont
فيرمونت دبي
DUBAI

HOTEL ACCOMMODATION AND SERVICES

LOCATION

Situated on the Sheikh Zayed Road in Dubai, directly opposite the Dubai World Trade Centre and in the heart of the business district.

    20 minutes to Dubai International Airport
    20 minutes to Dubai Media/Internet City
    Valet, indoor and outdoor parking for 650 vehicles

ACCOMMODATION

394 hotel rooms and suites

    266 deluxe hotel rooms with king and twin styles
    122 suites in combinations of one and two bedrooms
    6 two and three bedroom Penthouse Suites
    Fairmont Gold Floors with private check-in and lounge

DINING

12 Dining and Entertainment Venues
    Bridges Bar
    Spectrum on One, interactive dining featuring
    8 cuisines and 4 private rooms
    The Bar at Spectrum on One
    Cascades, 24 hour restaurant serving Mediterranean
    inspired cuisine
    Caffè Pronto
    The Exchange, elegant grill restaurant with 3 private rooms
    The Cigar Bar
    The Exchange Business Floor Lounge
    Sol Juice Bar
    Bacchus, Al Forno Restaurant
    Club
    Room Service, 24 hours

FEATURES

Willow Stream spa & health club
    Ladies' and men's treatment rooms
    Saunas, Steam Rooms, Jacuzzis and relaxation rooms
    2 terrace swimming pools with sun decks
    Aerobic, cardiovascular and fitness areas

The Exchange Business Floor
    State-of-the-art business centre
    2 meeting rooms
    4 private working cubicles
    3 Executive Boardrooms

PO Box 97555, Sheikh Zayed Road, Dubai, UAE
Tel: 971 4 332 5555 Fax: 971 4 332 4555 Email: dubai.sales@fairmont.com
Toll Free: UAE 800 4772 Kuwait & Qatar 971 4 311 8200 Saudi Arabia 800 897 1404 Bahrain 800 036

www.fairmont.com

Words themselves can only begin to portray the scope of the change, but the pictures of Noor Ali Rashid tell the story in a way that is immediately comprehensible, even if, at the same time, the changes themselves may sometimes seem almost unbelievable.

The purpose of this book is two-fold. At one level, the intention of Noor Ali Rashid is to inform and to educate today's residents of the United Arab Emirates about the scale of the changes that have taken place, which have lifted it from an underdeveloped economic country to a valued place in the community of nations.

At a second level, however, it is a celebration of that change, and of Noor Ali Rashid's own good fortune of being upon the scene and of being in the privileged position of being able to record the change.

The individual images are powerful, sometimes simply recording events, and sometimes almost works of art in themselves. Collectively, they paint a picture which offers convincing evidence of the process of the emergence of the UAE today. They do not pretend to look at everything, but, through the lens and the eye of the photographer, they paint a picture which is both remarkable and compelling. Many observers would say that nothing less of a description is appropriate for the story of the United Arab Emirates itself.

◆ ◆ ◆

Sheikh Ahmed bin Rashid Al Mualla, Ruler of Umm Al Quwain and Sheikh Rashid bin Humaid Al Nuaimi, Ruler of Ajman, were presented with ceremonial guns in 1961 by Political Resident Sir George Middleton, in the presence of Donald Hawley, Political Agent Dubai, at the Trucial Oman Scouts headquarters in Sharjah.

Sheikh Zayed bin Sultan Al Nahyan, Ruler of Abu Dhabi and now also President of the United Arab Emirates, in discussion with the Commander of the Trucial Oman Scouts and an Arab Officer at Sharjah Military base.

THE BRITISH FIRST came to the Gulf in the early 17th century, when Iran, under its old name of Persia, was a leading power in the region. In 1619 the Emperor, Shah Abbas, granted the British East India Company a monopoly of his country's silk trade and allowed its factors to settle at the Persian port of Bandar Abbas. For a century and a half the Company, a sturdy offshoot of its Bombay headquarters, gradually eclipsed its European rivals in the area and extended its commercial dominance northward to Basra. But whilst the Company prospered the empire of the Shahs declined and by the late 18th century threats to the Company's supremacy were appearing from all directions – the Afghans had invaded Persia from the east, disrupting internal trade routes; on the western side of the Gulf the coastal Arabs had destroyed the Persian footholds; in the north the Russians were active; and to the south the increasing power of the Qawasim was a cause for British concern. As so often happened, the British preoccupation with the protection of trade routes led to continuing extension of imperial control, and eventual British domination of the region.

Previous pages: A very different world. The British Political Resident inspecting a Royal Air Force parade in Sharjah in the early 60s.

The evening of Empire. Sir George Middleton (left), the British Political Resident in Bahrain, responsible for the entire Gulf region, and Donald Hawley, the Political Agent in Dubai, dressed in ceremonial No. 1s at the main gate of the Political Agency, prior to their departure for an official ceremony.

An early meeting of the Trucial States Council at the Political Agency in Dubai. From left to right: Sheikh Khalid bin Sultan Al Nahyan; Sheikh Rashid bin Saeed Al Maktoum, Ruler of Dubai; a suitably behatted Colonel Sir Hugh Boustead, the Political Agent in Abu Dhabi; Sheikh Shakhbut bin Sultan Al Nahyan, then Ruler of Abu Dhabi and James Craig, Political Agent in Dubai.

THE HORMUZ STRAITS were crucial to the trade between India, Persia, Mesopotamia and Europe – a fact well appreciated by the Qawasim who sought both to limit foreign intervention in the area as well as exact tolls on shipping passing through the straits. With settlements on both sides of the waterway they were in a good position to do so. Britain had secured part of the Arabian Sea coast through an alliance with the Seyyids of Muscat, but reached no such agreement with the Qawasim, whose response to what they considered to be increasing British intrusion was a sustained and, from the British point of view, an all-too-successful naval campaign. Although a treaty was signed in 1806 by Sheikh Sultan bin Saqr Al Qassimi, in which it was agreed that the Qawasim would no longer molest British ships (but, in a neat get-out clause, promised to give three months' notice should they change their mind!) it was short-lived. The attacks resumed with increasing ferocity – even seizing ships within 60 miles of Bombay. In 1819 the British responded with bombardments of the coastal Qawasim strongholds and the destruction of the fort at Ras Al Khaimah.

A time of change. From left to right: Kenneth Timbrell, Commanding Officer, British Troops in Sharjah; Sheikh Maktoum bin Rashid Al Maktoum, Crown Prince – now Ruler – of Dubai; Julian Bullard, Political Agent and Group Captain Max Scamell.

Sheikh Zayed with Donald Hawley who came to Abu Dhabi to bid him farewell at the end of his posting in Dubai. Also seen here is Mana Mohammed Al Dhaheri.

Ali Bustani and Donald Hawley enjoy Noor Ali's hospitality on the occasion of Eid.

THE IMMEDIATE RESULT of these fierce encounters was, in 1820, the first of a series of treaties and truces which marked the beginning of Britain's long links with the region. As time passed what had been called by fearful seafarers the Pirate Coast became known as the Trucial States. In 1823 the first Residency Agent was appointed in Sharjah, reporting to the British Political Resident in Bushire, and throughout the 19th century there was increasing British involvement in the affairs of the area. In 1853 a treaty of Perpetual Maritime Peace was concluded with local rulers and for the rest of the century there were flurries of understandings, treaties, assurances, agreements and memoranda which included a promise, in 1887, that the Trucial States would on no account correspond with or enter into an agreement with any government other than the British, nor would they, without the consent of the British Government, allow any agent of any other government to reside in their land. In 1892, in what became known as the 'Exclusive Agreement', the sheikhs also agreed not to cede, sell, mortgage or otherwise give for occupation any part of their territory save to the British Government.

Peter Lorrimer, first British Commandant of Dubai Police.

Overleaf: Cannon versus cavalry.

After attending a military parade, VIP guests pose for the camera: from left, Ebrahim Al Midfa, Sheikh Humaid bin Rashid Al Nuaimi, Crown Prince – and now Ruler – of Ajman, Saif bin Ahmed Rehman, Sheikh Mohammed bin Hamad Al Sharqi, Ruler of Fujairah, Sheikh Hamdan bin Rashid Al Maktoum, Colonel Bartholomew, Commander of the Trucial Oman Scouts (TOS), Sheikh Saqr bin Mohammed Al Qassimi, Ruler of Ras Al Khaimah, Donald Hawley, Sheikh Ahmed bin Rashid Al Mualla, Ruler of Umm Al Quwain, and his son, Sheikh Humaid bin Ahmed Al Mualla.

THE PAX BRITANNICA had arrived, at least at sea, and whilst Britain in theory had no control over the internal matters of the sheikhdoms it was inevitable that her representatives would get involved in various aspects of the administration if British commercial interests were to be served – which was, of course, the reason for the presence in the first place. It was an adage of the imperialists that trade always follows the flag – but in fact the opposite was more often true, with political and military influence following on to protect trading activities.

During the late 1920s and early 30s there were negotiations with the sheikhs – at meetings probably not dissimilar to those pictured here – to obtain landing and refuelling facilities for the aircraft of Imperial Airways en route to and from India. Eventually agreement was reached with Sharjah – and subsequently Dubai and Abu Dhabi – for the HP42s and Empire flying boats to call.

From the left: RAF Officer, Sheikh Rashid bin Humaid Al Nuaimi, Ruler of Ajman, the Commander of the TOS, Sharjah, Sheikh Mubarak bin Mohammed Al Nahyan and a TOS Officer.

Sheikh Ahmed of Umm Al Quwain offers hospitality to the Political Resident, Donald Hawley, Political Agent, and Ali Bustani, Assistant to the Political Agent.

An early meeting of the Trucial States Development Council held in Dubai. Sheikh Saqr bin Mohammed Al Qassimi of Ras Al Khaimah, first chairman of the TSDC, accompanied by Political Agent D. A. Roberts and legal adviser Ahmed Bitar.

BY 1935 THE search for oil had commenced on the Trucial Coast and, although this was not to produce results until nearly 25 years later, the idea alone was enough to impel change. After the Second World War the increasing British interest in the area led to greater political involvement in the region, including the setting up, in 1952, of the Trucial States Council, under the chairmanship of the Political Agent and designed to further co-operation between the rulers. It had no executive powers, but provided a useful consultative and advisory role. It was later complemented by the Trucial States Development Council, whose first chairman was Sheikh Saqr bin Mohammed Al Qassimi of Ras Al Khaimah. The second and last chairman was Sheikh Khalid bin Mohammed Al Qassimi, Ruler of Sharjah.

At first the development budget consisted primarily of British aid but, when Sheikh Zayed assumed power in Abu Dhabi in 1966, he provided an influx of funding that, long before the establishment of the UAE, helped to secure the mutual goodwill that was to form the bedrock of the new country.

The issue of visas was in the hands of the British administration, namely the Passport Officer who also provided additional public services for the expatriate citizens of the Commonwealth. Many people from the Trucial States region were issued with a British passport to enable them to travel to Britain and the Far East, giving them the status of British protected persons. In the 1960s though each emirate started to issue its own passports.

On the occasion of opening The British Trade Office in Deira, Dubai. From left to right: Ali Bustani, Majid Al Futtaim, Mohammed Hadi Badri, Ali Al Owais, Ahmed Al Ghurair, Nasir bin Abdul Latif, Donald Hawley, Sheikh Rashid, The British Commercial Officer, Hamad Al Futtaim, Haj Ghulam Abbas Ansari, Kamaz Hamza, Abdul Hai and Abdullah Hussain.

Standing to attention at the guard post of the Abu Dhabi Police headquarters.

THE TRUCIAL OMAN Levies were formed in 1951 to maintain law and order throughout the territory (except in the towns, where the Rulers' guards undertook police and security duties, and where the Levies were permitted to operate only with the sheikh's permission). They provided a local force whose members were largely composed of nationals rather than British troops. Sheikh Zayed in particular supported the concept and encouraged his people to enlist. Commanded by British officers, assisted by others from Jordan and Aden, the force, which changed its name to the Trucial Oman Scouts in 1956, also provided training for the police and the military of individual emirates.

Members of 5 Squadron and HQ Support Group at Sharjah. By the standards of the time they were a well-equipped force, their arsenal including machine guns and three mortars.

Cadets at the Trucial Oman Scouts Boys School. Mainly for sons of serving soldiers, the school provided one of the relatively few educational opportunities.

THE TOS, IN conjunction with British military units based in the emirates, also undertook a variety of civilian roles including blasting tracks through the Hajar Mountains (long since superseded by fine modern highways, but traces of which may still be seen clinging to precipitous hillsides), surveying on behalf of the Trucial States Development Council and running an emergency ambulance and evacuation service.

By 1971 the TOS had nearly 1,400 members, including over 30 Arab officers, and formed the nucleus of what, on independence, was to become the Union Defence Force – although both Dubai and Abu Dhabi continued to maintain separate forces in addition for some years after federation.

A group photograph of Arab soldiers with their commander, Col. Carter, at their Sharjah headquarters.

Students and teachers of the Trade School, Sharjah.

THE TRUCIAL OMAN Scouts also provided an educational function – at a time when schools were uncommon in the region – by language and trade training. Until then education had been obtained either through the *mutawa* Koranic schools or by travelling overseas – mainly to Bahrain, Iraq or Kuwait. The first modern school in the region opened in Sharjah in 1953 – followed just a year later by a school for girls, a revolutionary step in a deeply traditional society.

Whilst the Sharjah schools were pioneers and attracted pupils from all over the country, it was not long before other emirates instituted their own educational establishments – Dubai's first opened in 1957. Within 10 years there were 22 schools in the northern emirates with a total enrolment of some 5,000 pupils of whom around 1,500 were girls.

The Rulers of Sharjah and Fujairah, together with other Sheikhs, government officials and the Political Agent watching a school parade in Sharjah. The event seems to have been popular, judging by the crowds perched precariously on the roofs.

Sheikh Mohammed bin Khalid Al Qassimi, son of the late Ruler of Sharjah demonstrating his creative abilities at school in Sharjah. Artistic activity was positively encouraged, alongside the academic curriculum.

31

THE SHEIKHDOMS OF the Trucial Coast were the first Arab states into which Britain brought her authority – and the last which she was to leave in 1971. Although originally the importance of the area to the British was primarily to protect the route to the Indian Empire, after the Second World War the Gulf assumed a significance all of its own to Britain – much of the country's oil came from the region. But a new world was fast approaching, and an imperial system constructed for the first half of the 19th century was hardly suitable for the second half of the 20th. It could not last and, in 1968, the British Labour Government announced that Britain would withdraw from the region.

On the 1st of December, 1971 the British Resident flew down from Bahrain to the Trucial Coast for a final farewell tour by car and helicopter. To each ruler he went, armed with a flowery little speech in Arabic in one hand and a formal declaration of withdrawal in the other. Then, when all seven sheikhs had been visited and the final instrument of British renunciation had been signed, he left. He had worked himself – as well as the British Empire – out of a job.

On completion of a tour of duty by a commanding officer it was customary for the flag to be handed over to his successor. At the Trucial Oman Scouts headquarters in Sharjah Col. Stuart Carter is brought the flag by his personal attendant.

Conservative leader Edward Heath toured the Gulf in 1968 to assess the local reaction to the British troops' withdrawal announcement by the Labour Government. Here he meets Sheikh Mohammed bin Rashid Al Maktoum, now Crown Prince of Dubai, at a formal evening reception.

It was traditional for departing commanding officers to be towed off the base by their men rather than driven.

Sheikh Hamdan bin Mohammed Al Nahyan, centre, representing the Ruler of Abu Dhabi, Sheikh Zayed, at a meeting of the Trucial States Rulers held at the Al Diyafa Palace, Dubai. Also present, from the right: Sheikh Rashid of Dubai, Sheikh Saqr of Ras Al Khaimah, Sheikh Mohammed of Fujairah, Sheikh Khalid of Sharjah, Sheikh Ahmed of Umm Al Quwain and Sheikh Rashid of Ajman.

Previous pages: 2 December 1971 – a new nation is born. The shadow of the United Arab Emirates flag, which has just been hoisted by Sheikh Zayed and his fellow Rulers, flies for the first time, sweeping the ground of Dubai's Al Diyafa Palace. The Palace, also known as the Jumeirah Guest House, was renamed Dar Al Ittihad – the House of Unity – on the occasion of the nation's Silver Jubilee.

THE FIRST STEP on the road to federation was taken not in the Gulf but far away in London, where the government of the day was wrestling with the familiar post-war problem of reducing national expenditure. Then, as now, one of the first areas to be considered for cost cutting was the armed services and in early 1967 proposals were put forward for the closing of all military bases east of Suez – although, at that time, it was not intended to withdraw from the Gulf itself. Indeed in November 1967 assurances were still being given that the British armed forces would be maintained in the region, in accordance with the obligations of the treaty.

Federation meeting in progress in Abu Dhabi, at which Sheikh Zayed headed the discussions between the nine emirates, including Bahrain and Qatar, during the late 60s.

Sheikh Mohammed Al Sharqi, Ruler of Fujairah and his son, Sheikh Hamad bin Mohammed – now Ruler – wave as their guests leave the emirate.

Sheikh Zayed coming out of the Trucial
States Development Council Office at
Deira, Dubai after concluding a meeting
of the seven participating emirates in
the new federation.

Sheikh Zayed in close conference
with Sheikh Saqr of Ras Al
Khaimah during one of the
Accession Day celebrations in
Abu Dhabi.

HOWEVER, BY JANUARY 1968, to satisfy the party political requirements of domestic policy, the British Government had decided on a complete withdrawal of all troops east of Suez, including those based in the Gulf, by the end of 1971. Although initially it was hoped that with a change of government in Britain there might be a reversal of the decision this was not to be and it became obvious that the Trucial States, Bahrain and Qatar would have to assume all the responsibilities of independent nations. Whilst Britain, in theory at least, was responsible only for external affairs and defence, in practice British administrators had also become involved in domestic matters.

Sheikh Zayed at the wheel with Sheikh Mohammed of Fujairah, on a city drive.

Sheikh Khalifa bin Hamad Al Thani, Crown Prince of Qatar with Sheikh Rashid of Ajman, on a walkabout during a federation meeting of Crown Princes and Deputy Rulers at Ajman.

The Ruler of Qatar, Sheikh Ahmed bin Ali Al Thani, hosting a banquet at his palace in Dubai, amongst whose guests included the Rulers of Dubai, Sharjah, Umm Al Quwain and Ras Al Khaimah.

NEGOTIATIONS BETWEEN THE seven emirates and Bahrain and Qatar commenced with a meeting of the nine Rulers held in Dubai in late February 1968. The basis for the discussions flowed from the understanding reached by Sheikh Zayed and Sheikh Rashid at their historic meeting at As Sameeh earlier in that month at which they had decided to unite Abu Dhabi and Dubai in a federation. The fundamentals of that agreement were that federation would encompass defence, security, foreign affairs, immigration policies and social services. Although both Bahrain and Qatar eventually elected to become separate states, the seven rulers of the Trucial States continued their quest for equitable unity, culminating in an announcement on 18 July, 1971 of the formation of a new country – the United Arab Emirates.

Sheikh Zayed accompanied by Sheikh Rashid during National Day celebrations in Abu Dhabi.

Sheikh Ahmed of Umm Al Quwain leaving his palace and looking on as his personal guards run to bring his car.

2 December, 1971 – as Ahmed Khalifa Al Suwaidi reads the Rulers' statement on the launch of the new nation, Sheikh Zayed on behalf of the UAE and Sir Geoffrey Arthur on behalf of Britain, sign the first ever agreement to be entered into by the union. Bearing witness to this historic moment are Sheikh Rashid, Sheikh Khalid of Sharjah, Sheikh Maktoum, Sheikh Hamdan, Mehdi Al Tajir, Ibrahim Al Midfa and Sheikh Faisal bin Khalid Al Qassimi.

THE NEW STATE came into being on 2 December, 1971, when the rulers of Abu Dhabi, Dubai, Sharjah, Ajman, Umm Al Quwain and Fujairah signed the provisional constitution. Ras Al Khaimah, which had some reservations concerning its representation in the Council, did not join the federation until Febuary of the following year. At the first meeting of the Supreme Council Sheikh Zayed was elected President and Sheikh Rashid Vice-President and Prime Minister. The success of the new nation was not assured, but with the skills of its leaders and the goodwill of the international community, already it seemed that the scepticism with which its future had been viewed was misplaced.

The official line-up in February 1972 to commemorate Ras Al Khaimah joining the federation. Sheikh Sultan bin Mohammed Al Qassimi, second from left, had become Ruler of Sharjah on 25 January, succeeding his brother, Sheikh Khalid.

DEVELOPING
A NATION

Abu Dhabi in transition. When this photograph was taken in 1969 the shape that the modern city was to take was already visible. The Corniche had been completed and most of the other main roads were in place – but the towering forests of high-rise apartments and offices were yet to come.

JUST A GENERATION or so ago the towns and villages of the UAE were constructed solely of locally available materials. Whilst the popular perception of a typical Arab dwelling is that of a tent, a mobile home that followed the Bedu's migrations, they were never used to any great extent in the Emirates where most of the inhabitants led a more settled existence.

Along the coast many houses were built of coral blocks or the soft rock found along the shore. Inland, in places where there was a sufficient supply of water, mud bricks were used for the construction of homes and forts, the material being easy to work and allowing the builders to add intricate decorative patterns. In the mountains stone was more readily available and the houses, with stone-tiled or palm-frond roofs, were often partially dug into the ground which kept them cooler in summer and warmer in winter. Throughout the country *barasti* or *'arish* – the branches of palm trees – was used for temporary, movable dwellings as well as for fencing animal stockades, as it is still today.

Al Ain, in the early 1970s, was still a largely rural settlement with few tarmac roads. At the intersection of major trade routes and blessed with abundant water supplies the town had been an important agricultural and commercial centre for centuries.

Previous pages: An ageless scene on the Sharjah shoreline. The design of the boats and the ritual of mending the nets has changed little since men first put to sea.

Curving through the heart of the town, Dubai's creek has been compared to the Grand Canal in Venice. Certainly the Venetian concept of a city-state founded on international trade is one with which Dubai is familiar.

THE RAPID GROWTH in the years following the formation of the UAE turned the cities into vast building sites as the foundations of a modern infrastructure were laid. Roads, power supplies, telephones, street lights, drainage and all the other paraphernalia of a 20th-century environment had to be put in place.

One of the most important difficulties that had to be addressed as the cities expanded was the growing demand for water. Less than 30 per cent of the country's total water requirement can be met by traditional sources – wells, dams and the *falaj* which tap underground supplies and carry the water through tunnels several kilometres long. In any event the area's low rainfall and high rate of evaporation makes natural water a rapidly depletable resource. The sea – which for so long provided a means of trade and communications, a source of wealth and a mainstay of the diet – is now the prime source of fresh water, created by desalination plants which supply the increasing demands of industry, agriculture and the population itself.

The prominent reference point of Sharjah's clocktower in the late 60s, which later was to draw the urban landscape nearer like a magnet.

Overleaf: Abu Dhabi's historic landmark of Al Husn Fort.

IT IS ESTIMATED that in the early 1970s there were some 60,000 homes in the UAE; by the mid-90s that had increased to in excess of 400,000, more than 100,000 of which have been built by the government and given free of charge to the more needy citizens. Many are in rural areas where new villages have been built – bringing to the inhabitants the advantages of schools, power supplies and health services.

Although many of the original properties have been pulled down, to make way for new construction, throughout the country houses built of traditional materials may still be seen. Occasionally the old has been adapted and a purring air-conditioning unit jutting from a mud-brick wall offers a pleasing sense of continuity.

Cement for the huge construction programme initiated by Sheikh Zayed had to be imported before local manufacturing plants were built. Here thousands of tons lie awaiting distribution.

Many of the houses in Bur Dubai were ornately decorated with traditional motifs – coffee pots being a familiar theme. This was the office of Cable and Wireless Ltd.

In the early 1960s many of the old buildings in Dubai and other emirates were demolished to make way for modern development. Fortunately some survived this initial frenzy of activity and many have now been restored.

Before the construction of modern port facilities imported goods had to be unloaded on the foreshore, as here on what was to become Abu Dhabi's Corniche.

ALONG ABU DHABI'S Corniche and Dubai's creek there were rising office blocks, banks, hotels and other buildings that were to so dramatically alter not only the appearance of the cities but the way of life of their inhabitants, providing facilities and services that few could have imagined even a few years before.

Whilst the main centres of activity were concentrated on the cities, throughout the country plans were being laid for the construction of roads and bridges, ports and airports, hospitals and schools, desalination plants and sewage systems, power stations and distribution grids.

Wood to be used in construction piled high on Abu Dhabi's Corniche.

Overleaf: the soft light over Deira highlights the barasti settlements which nestle in snugly with the low-lying villas.

Many of Dubai's administrative buildings were situated along the banks of the creek. Originally built as a residence and diwan for Sheikh Saeed in 1954, when he moved from Beit Saeed in Shindagah, the building in the foreground later also housed the Customs Office, warehouses and a primary school.

DUBAI'S CREEK HAS always formed both the visual and commercial focal point of the city – or, more properly, of the two cities of Dubai and Deira.

The creek, one of the few natural harbours on the southern coast of the Gulf, is the reason for Dubai's existence and has for centuries provided a safe haven for dhows – and, more recently, for vessels serving the offshore oil rigs. From here pearlers would head out to the great pearl banks in the draining heat of summer – hardy men indeed, these, making up to 50 dives a day, living on a frugal diet of dates, fish, rice and coffee and towing their fresh water in huge tubs behind them. Merchants dispatched their vessels from the creek, as they do today, venturing to East Africa, India and the Far East in search of trade. And gold by the ton left from these shores to satisfy India's constant demand for the precious metal.

Some commodities never made it as far as the markets and were sold as soon as they were unloaded.

Sharjah fort was the official residence of the Ruler until 1965. It then became the headquarters of Sharjah Police and was demolished to make way for the new banking centre.

IN THE NEIGHBOURING emirate of Sharjah there was rapid development too. The little souk and scattering of houses that straggled along the side of the town's creek was home, in 1960, to around 5,000 people. Just a decade later there was a population of over 20,000 – and by current estimates is now more than 330,000.

At the beginning of the 20th century Sharjah was the most important port in the southern Gulf. Apart from its creek, it was the first town in the emirates to have an airport, opened in 1932, and for more than a century it housed the only British political representative in the region, until the opening of a political agency in Dubai in 1954.

But by the 1950s silting of the creek, upon which so much of the town's prosperity depended, had virtually closed the entrance and the ships had moved to Dubai. It was not until the 1970s that Sharjah's creek was dredged and a new port – the first in the Middle East to take container cargoes – was constructed.

By the early 70s the pace of life was beginning to quicken. The branches of the tree overhanging the road belong to the Rola tree, which, to Sharjah residents, marked the centre of Sharjah's business district, the main taxi stand, and a place of gathering for Eid festivities.

Al Khan, Sharjah. Watchtowers were a common feature of towns and villages and there are still dozens of them dotted around the country, guardians of shorelines, hills and mountain passes.

61

THE PACE OF progress was more leisurely in the north and east of the country, where the traditional occupations of fishing and farming are still part of daily life. It was not always so. The fort at Umm Al Quwain received the attention of the British in 1820 although there was no evidence of any complicity in the attacks on shipping; and the French, in 1891, attempted to solicit alliances with the Ruler – leading to the Exclusive Agreement of 1892, whereby it was agreed that the sheikhs would not cede, sell, mortgage or otherwise give for occupation any part of their territory, save to the British Government.

Fujairah, on the east coast, was sleepier still. In the mid-1970s the list of subscribers in its one-page telephone directory numbered ten.

Visions of change: a serene landscape framed within an elegant archway at Fujairah Palace.

Typical of defensive architecture in the region, the fort at Umm Al Quwain has the protruding beak-like machicolations that enabled marksmen to fire almost vertically downwards. It was, until recently, when it was converted into a museum, used as a police post.

Fujairah's fort, standing atop a rocky knoll, was the Ruler's residence until the late 1950s. Built of mud on a stone base, it was surrounded by the modest houses of the population – who, like their Ruler, have now abandoned the old for the comforts of more modern dwellings.

Khor Fakkan's wide bay has provided a haven for seafarers ever since the first days of Arab navigation. Now the fishermen share their handsome harbour with a busy container port from which goods are distributed throughout Arabia.

THE BATINA COAST, because of its position facing the Indian Ocean, was more exposed to the attention of sea-powers and, as a result, its history is better documented than the Gulf shores. The Arab geographer, Masudi, records that sailors from here brought the 'orange' from the Far East to the Batina, whence it was first introduced to Europe. Down the centuries many nations squabbled over the area: Omanis sacked Khor Fakkan 1,000 years ago; the north-east monsoon brought the Portuguese here from Mozambique in the early 16th century; the Ottomans sailed south from Basra; the Persians crossed the Gulf to obtain a foothold. But shifting patterns of trade and power saw international interest in the area decline and by the beginning of the 19th century there were just a few small fishing villages with the occasional fort brooding over them.

Now, with fine new roads slicing through the Hajar mountains, the Batina provides a pleasant break for the city dwellers of the west coast – and visitors from further afield – who come to admire the handsome scenery and relax on the beaches.

Fujairah, for so long isolated from the other emirates by the formidable barrier of the Hajar mountains, is now growing rapidly, its population having increased almost ten-fold from its late-60s total of 7,900.

BUSINESS
AND INDUSTRY

Previous pages: The manufacture
of pottery is one of the earliest
human achievements in this region,
dating back some 5,000 years.

Trap nets or gargours may still be
seen at almost any fishing port in
the Gulf. They are dropped over the
side of dhows and their position
marked, these days, by brightly
coloured polystyrene blocks or
plastic containers finding a new
lease of life as floats.

FISHING HAS BEEN an important source of both income and protein for centuries. On both east and west coasts the fishermen, their lives governed by the steady rhythm of the tides, have put forth in search of their catch. The waters of the UAE harbour rich stocks – although, as in other parts of the world, recent overfishing has put some species under pressure.

For deeper waters the dhow is used, but inshore fishing is often undertaken in a *shasha*, a small boat fashioned from the ubiquitous palm-frond. Trap nets or *gargours* – shaped like igloos into which the fish would swim and then be unable to escape – are still a common sight, either piled along the shoreline or stacked aboard dhows. Purse seine nets are also used, being dropped over the side and then their throats being drawn closed. Whilst fishing continues year round the best season is between September and May when cooler, less saline water flows in from the Indian Ocean, replenishing stocks.

In the days before refrigeration fresh fish were available only on the coast. Inland the inhabitants had to make do with a malodorous, dried version.

The shasha is one of the world's oldest seacrafts and has its equivalent in Africa, South America and Asia. This one was photographed at Fujairah, where contemporary versions still make small voyages.

This street vendor in Umm Al Quwain has a small but eclectic range of goods.

Previous pages: Apart from the
outboard motors there
is nothing in this photograph that
would appear unusual
to a time-travelling fisherman –
from whatever century he may
have come.

NOWHERE IS THE tradition of trade more obviously displayed than in the souks. It was customary for different occupations or commodities to cluster together in particular areas – and even today shoppers head for the gold souk, the fish market or the spice souk to make their purchases. The souks have always played a vital role in business – much more than mere shops, they were, and to some extent still are, miniature commodity exchanges. Imported goods – rice, coffee, cloth, pots, pans and dozens of other staples – would be sold; dates, horses, shark fins, limes and other items would be exported.

Traders of all kinds of merchandise were at liberty by the municipality to sell their many wares on the street without the financial burden of stall rental. From leather to lace, goods were generally of bargain basement value which meant a quick profit, much to the displeasure of the official stallholders within the souk!

Water was, even in the changing times of the city, an ever precious commodity and mules were the simplest bearers for delivery to people's homes.

73

DIFFERENT TRADES HAD different etiquettes. Pearl traders would never discuss price openly and negotiations would follow an ancient ritual, although one based on practical good sense. The seller would deal with a number of bidders by touching hands beneath a cloth: thus negotiations could be undertaken between several parties at the same time, yet no buyer could know what other bids had been made.

Whilst each of the souks had its own fascination – from the tumultuous colours of the textile market to the heady, pungent aromas of the spice souk – it was gold, or the Indian passion for the metal, that made many of Dubai's early fortunes. In 1947 the Indian Government, concerned by the drain on its foreign exchange holdings, banned the importation of gold. Enterprising merchants would purchase bullion on the markets of London and Zurich and have it air-freighted to Dubai, 200 four-ounce ingots to a box. It would then be shipped to India, the trade only becoming illicit when the cargo entered Indian waters. At its peak the value of gold imported into Dubai was of the order of 400 million dollars a year. It was ironic that it was the oil crisis of the early 70s that brought the trade to an end. Global inflation created such a demand for the metal that ordinary Indians could no longer afford it and by the end of 1973 the business was over.

The contrast between the newly-arrived telephone and the old-fashioned scales neatly summarises a period of transition.

Despite gold's obvious attraction, there was still a strong demand for imitation jewellery.

Tea chests, wicker baskets and barasti roofs were the basic requirements of setting up shop in the souk.

The Abu Dhabi Ruler's Representative, Mubarak bin Hadhr, amidst the bleak landscape of Das Island.

WHILST THE GOLD trade may have declined, save for local sales, oil revenues more than made up for it. The first oil to be exported from what was to become the UAE was in 1962 from Abu Dhabi's offshore Umm Shaif Field. Ten years later Dubai's first field started exporting – and in that year the production value of oil exports from the country as a whole reached 4,500 million dirhams. By 1992 that had increased more than twelve-fold to 57,241 million dirhams – although production itself had less than doubled from 1.22 million barrels per day to 2.15 million. Proven reserves – using current techniques of recovery – are now conservatively estimated to be in excess of 100 billion barrels, compared with the 32.7 billion barrels estimate made in the late 70s.

But such heady numbers were still speculation in Dubai in the early 1960s. Certainly surveys had indicated that oil was present, but it was not until 1967 that Dubai Petroleum Company started production from the offshore Fateh Field.

Sheikh Rashid, accompanied by the chairman and other executives from Continental Oil Company (Conoco), Mehdi Al Tajir (extreme left of picture) and Sheikh Maktoum, prior to their departure to an onshore rig by helicopter.

Sheikh Rashid and Sheikh Mohammed pictured at the Margham oilfield.

Sheikh Khalid bin Mohammed
Al Qassimi, Ruler of Sharjah,
signs an agreement for oil
exploration with officials from the
Crescent Oil Company. To Sheikh
Khalid's right is Nadim Pachachi.
The event is witnessed by
prominent Sharjah dignitaries.

Sheikh Saqr bin Sultan Al Qassimi
accompanied by Sheikh Ali Bin
Rashid Al Nuaimi and other
officials inspect a drilling rig near
Abu Musa Island.

NINETY KILOMETRES OFFSHORE and 2,300 metres deep, Dubai's Fateh Field may not be huge in production terms but it deserves a place of honour in the petroleum Hall of Fame for its *khazzans*. The word in Arabic means, prosaically, storage – but these are no ordinary containers. Each high enough to cover a 15-storey building they stand like upturned champagne glasses on the sea-bed. They work on a simple principle of science – oil and water do not mix – and, better yet, oil floats on water. Oil is pumped into the *khazzan*, displacing the sea-water; tankers remove the oil from the top of the *khazzan*, the sea-water rising accordingly.

Each *khazzan's* capacity is some 20 million gallons and each weighs, empty, 15,000 tons. They have a diameter of 82 metres and a height of 62 metres which, with the sea-bed being 47 metres deep, leaves some 15 metres above the surface. Obviating the need to pump crude 90 kilometres to shore for storage – and then out to a deep-water loading bay – they enabled offshore production to be carried at the best place for it: offshore.

The Chicago Iron and Steel Company (which prefabricated the component parts of the *khazzans* and shipped them piecemeal to the UAE where they were assembled at the western end of the village of Jumeirah) may be gratified to know that they have lent their name to one of the Middle East's most prestigious leisure developments – Chicago Beach.

Sheikh Rashid being presented with a model of a khazzan.

The real khazzan, of which this is just a small part, dwarfs a team of visitors led by Sheikh Rashid at the construction site.

At the opening of the British Bank of the Middle East's new office in Dubai, 1964. Sir Dallas Bernard, Chairman of the BBME (sitting, centre) with the branch's staff, including (sitting, left to right) B.W.J.S. Brisby, Manager Designate, J.C. Kelly, Manager Dubai and Easa Saleh Al Gurg, Commercial Manager.

THE DEVELOPING INFRASTRUCTURE required more than roads and buildings. For most of the century the Indian rupee had been the currency in use in the Trucial States (indeed one of the *abra* crossings in Dubai is still referred to as the two-anna *abra*), occasionally substituted by the chunky Maria Theresa dollar. When the rupee was devalued in 1966 Abu Dhabi adopted the Bahraini dinar and Qatar issued the Qatar-Dubai riyal, with the result that the UAE came into being with two currencies.

The first bank to open in the region was the British Bank of the Middle East's Dubai office in 1946, the company also being the first bank in Abu Dhabi, where it opened in 1959. The National Bank of Dubai was founded in 1963, and the National Bank of Abu Dhabi in 1968. It was not until 1973 that the UAE Currency Board (later to evolve into the Central Bank of the UAE) was set up to establish the national currency.

International banks soon realised the potential and established a presence – by 1974 there were 19 foreign banks operating in the UAE as well as seven locally incorporated institutions. Six years later this had grown to a total of 50 and, as an acknowledgement of the area's financial importance, the Arab Monetary Fund was based in Abu Dhabi.

Sheikh Zayed with Ahmed bin Sulayem and Khalaf Al Otaiba at the opening in 1968 of the National Bank of Abu Dhabi.

The opening of the National Bank of Dubai's branch in Umm Al Quwain in 1966. Banking in the modern sense was still fairly new and the opening of a new office something of a state occasion. Here the Ruler and Crown Prince of Umm Al Quwain are joined by dignitaries and businessmen from Umm Al Quwain and Dubai.

Leading members of the community in Dubai: from left, Ahmed Al Ghurair, Ali Al Owais and Hamad Al Futtaim.

AS THE ECONOMY developed so did the demand for consumer goods and services – and the opportunities to satisfy it. Early entrants into local production were manufacturers of soft drinks – hardly surprising in a climate where the summer temperatures could reach the high 40 degrees centigrade and at a time when air-conditioning was not so ubiquitous as it was later to become.

Increasing business activity and the burgeoning numbers of expatriate workers who wanted to keep in touch with home also required additional services and the introduction of efficient telephone and mail services became a priority.

Abu Dhabi's first stamp was issued in 1963, but before then several other emirates had sold stamp rights and the result was a series of colourful philatelic oddities. The gentleman in this photograph was the postmaster in Dubai and might have disapproved of such issues as Fujairah's 'Stars of the Silver Screen' series. In 1972 there were 5,000 post office boxes in the UAE; just 20 years later that had increased to more than 94,000.

Sheikh Maktoum is shown round a Coca-Cola bottling plant.

TRANSPORT
THE KEY TO TRADE

Whilst the creek is the beginning and end of journeys that have taken Arab traders to India, East Africa, the Spice Islands of Indonesia and China as well as the ports of the Gulf, it is also the origin and destination of smaller voyages. Abras – Dubai's busy water-taxis – were the only way of crossing the creek until the Maktoum Bridge was opened in 1963.

Previous pages: Cargo and fishing boats moored along Umm Al Quwain's shoreline, renowned for being the transit centre for trade.

THE CENTRE OF activity in Dubai has always been the creek. From the wind-towered houses whose walls were lapped by the waters of the tidal inlet that provided the reason for the city's existence, Dubai's merchants could keep a watchful eye on the movement of their cargoes. They had plenty to observe: *abras* busily fussing across the water, linking the twin towns of Deira and Dubai; cargoes being loaded and unloaded on quays; boats being repaired on sandy foreshores; and the constant movement of dhows slipping in and out with the tides.

In many ways not much has changed. The creek is still the vigorous hub of the city and, although there are now modern bulk and container ports that handle some of the world's largest vessels, much local and regional trade is still transported by dhow.

Donald Hawley and Sir George Middleton seen leaving the jetty of the Political Agency, on the Bur Dubai side of the creek.

Abras required specialised craftsmanship. Nearly all are now motorised but in the 1950s and 60s most still relied on the muscle-power of the oarsman.

Abras encouraged potential customers to flow between the choice of bustling souks situated on either bank of the creek.

IT WAS NOT only cargo that travelled by dhow. Before the aircraft became the prime means of international transport most passengers arrived in or departed from Dubai by sea. Whilst the journeys within the Gulf were comparatively easy, the longer trips to India and East Africa were, for passengers, something of an ordeal, there being few facilities on board.

Dhow is, in fact, a word unknown in Arabic, being Anglicised from the Swahili term for any lateen-rigged vessel. Arabs identify their boats with much more precise terminology – *sanbuk* or *boom* or *baghlah*. Boat building was for many years one of the few manufacturing industries in Dubai, the wood usually being imported from India, the ropes from East Africa and the canvas for sails from Bahrain.

Heavily silted at mid-century, few vessels of any size could gain entrance to Sharjah's creek. Now dredged – and with the additional facilities at Port Khalid – Sharjah's import and export trade is again flourishing.

Sheikh Rashid's humanitarian efforts helped a large number of Haj pilgrims, who, when their launch capsized at the mouth of Dubai's creek were flown back to their homes in Pakistan by specially-chartered flights.

FROM 1904 THE British India Steam Navigation Company called at Dubai fortnightly, on its regular route from Bombay to Basra, bringing passengers and cargo to the emirate. Before the construction of Port Rashid the B&I ships would anchor a mile or so off the coast, passengers and cargo being unloaded into Gray Mackenzie's lighters for the last small leg of their voyage. Cargo would be winched over the side into the waiting barges but gangways were lowered for passengers – an easy enough transition in calm weather but more difficult when the sea was choppy.

A precarious arrival.

Compared with the ease of disembarking from an aircraft the transfer from ship to barge to shore was a complex procedure.

Police and immigration officials would travel out on the barge to meet arriving ships.

Four-wheel drive vehicles were, apart from the camel, the best way to travel around the country – and even that had its difficulties.

APART FROM A few streets in the centre of Dubai there were no tarmac roads anywhere else in the country until 1965. Even before the announcement of British withdrawal from the area the Trucial States Council had given high priority to the improvement of communications between the emirates and for many years road construction was the biggest single item on the Council's budget. The Dubai-Sharjah road was opened by Sheikh Saqr bin Mohammed of Ras Al Khaimah, Chairman of the Council, in 1966, and the highway was subsequently extended to Ras Al Khaimah in 1969. Abu Dhabi and Dubai were not linked by a surfaced road until after federation. As for journeys to the east coast, until the opening of the road through the mountains in the 1970s, most travellers elected to go by boat around the tip of the Musandam peninsula rather than face the long, arduous journey by gravel tracks through the wadis and defiles of the Hajar mountains.

The introduction of surfaced roads brought the benefits of the developing economy to even the most remote settlements.

By the fort at Umm Al Quwain. Land Rovers, more than 30 years on, appear much the same as they did then; the finned American car looks much more dated.

THE ARRIVAL OF roads brought significant economic and social benefits to the entire country – and particularly to rural areas. The produce of the developing agricultural areas especially at Digdaga in Ras Al Khaimah and at Al Ain, could be quickly taken to the emerging markets of the cities; imported foods, even perishables, could be swiftly transported throughout the land; medical and other social services could be more easily brought to the people of the interior; and material for the construction of new homes and other buildings could be cost-effectively distributed.

There were other less immediately obvious but equally important advantages, particularly after federation: the people became able to move about their new country and learn about their neighbours, fostering a sense of unity, developing business links and helping to knit the formerly disparate emirates into a truly unified whole.

The new port facilities that were being built in several of the emirates, enabled the easier import of raw materials for road construction.

Overleaf: At Sharjah Military Airport the guard of honour was frequently on parade, to welcome or bid farewell to Political Agents and Commanders of the TOS or the Royal Air Force.

Occasionally, VIPs from Aden, Bahrain and Oman visited the RAF camp in Sharjah, aboard such aircraft as this RAF Hunting Percival Pembroke.

FOR THE PEOPLE of the Gulf, where land transport was difficult and shipping services infrequent, air travel became immediately popular. Pearl merchants, whose high value, low weight merchandise was ideally served by air, were able to sell their goods within days rather than weeks. Merchants were able to import fresh produce with ease – and sell it at a handsome profit. And Colonel Loch, the hitherto isolated Political Agent in Bahrain, commented that because of the air service they were in the world instead of out of it.

Regular services had come to Sharjah in 1932, when Imperial Airways was granted landing rights. Passengers were accommodated at Imperial's Rest House in Sharjah, now long since abandoned but amazingly still standing amongst the city's modern development. In this fortified hotel – complete with electric lights, fans, refrigerators, wireless and a searchlight so powerful that in clear conditions pilots could see its welcoming beam from a distance of 130 kilometres – travellers relaxed in comfort. The old airfield served Sharjah well for 45 years until the developing town threatened to surround it and a new airport was constructed, opening in 1977.

A Syrian Arab Airlines aircraft at Sharjah in the late 1960s. After the old Sharjah Airport closed the runway was incorporated into the city's road system – and a fine, broad highway it made.

Sheikh Khalifa bin Zayed, Abu Dhabi Crown Prince, accompanied by Sheikh Mubarak, inspects the guard of honour at Abu Dhabi Airport.

Dubai Airport in 1960, not long after it had opened. The aircraft, a Douglas DC-3, was one of the largest yet to have arrived.

ALTHOUGH A FLYING boat service utilising the creek was inaugurated in 1937, Dubai's first airport suitable for regular flights by landplanes did not open until 1960, its 1,800-metre compacted sand runway capable of handling aircraft up to the size of a DC-3. In its first year of operation there were 772 scheduled flights and some 10,000 passengers, but growth was rapid and in 1965 a new, paved, 2,800-metre runway was opened. Virtually continuous development since has enabled Dubai International Airport to handle its current total of some six million passengers a year.

In Abu Dhabi, Sheikh Shakhbut had agreed, somewhat reluctantly, to allow Britain's Imperial Airways to establish an emergency landing strip as long ago as 1934, but it was not until after the Second World War that aviation made any real progress in the emirate. The first visitors were the oil companies who, in the 1950s, constructed an airfield just a few kilometres out of town by grading and rolling a conveniently flat piece of desert. Amongst Sheikh Zayed's priorities when he came to power was the building of an airport of international standards at Bateen, which opened in 1968.

Sheikh Rashid is greeted by Julian Bullard, the British Political Agent in Dubai. He had arrived in a BAC 1-11 of Gulf Aviation, the forerunner of Gulf Air.

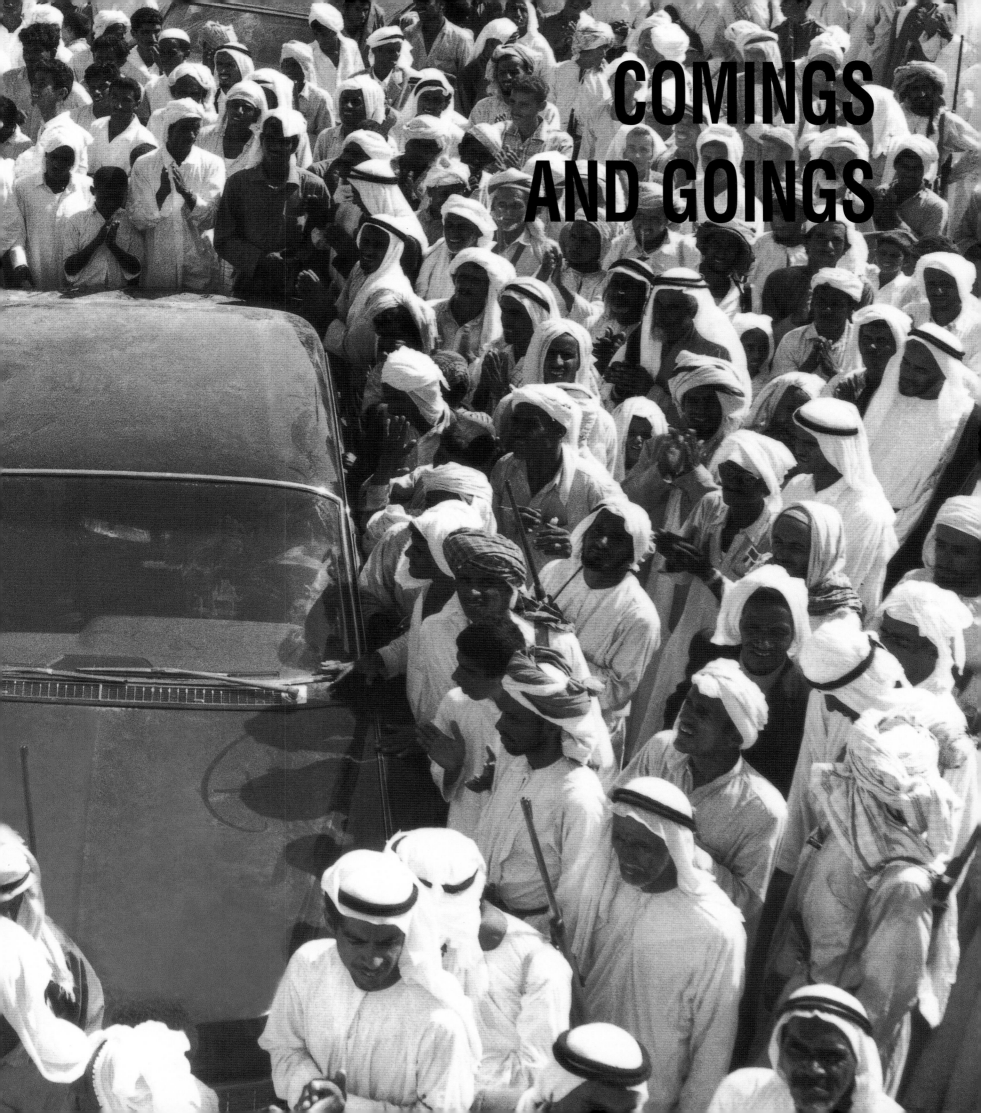

COMINGS
AND GOINGS

Laughing like brothers: Sheikh Rashid and Sheikh Zayed during Accession Day celebrations.

THE TRADITION OF Arab hospitality is reflected in the manner in which foreign dignitaries have been welcomed throughout the Emirates. Receptions of the highest calibre are laid on in the guest's honour, meals in the style of banquets are produced, and the cordial gathering of the traditional majlis is commonplace. These occasions are in keeping with domestic celebrations, where attention to detail is customary. The significance of these rituals runs deep, and is evidence of the tight links between the Rulers.

Of these domestic celebrations, the most momentous were those held on the anniversaries of Sheikh Zayed's Accession and on National Day. The marking of these events formed a point of focus for the new country, and helped to create a sense of national unity among its people.

Attending a 'durbar' in 1958 after Sheikh Rashid (seated) became the Ruler of Dubai, the British Political Agent and the Political Resident listen to Sheikh Maktoum's speech. It was the first photograph of the royal family that Noor Ali Rashid took.

Previous pages: The 1964 visit of the Arab League delegation generated – as here in Ras Al Khaimah – huge crowd gatherings.

Sheikh Zayed with his son Sheikh Hamdan in Lausanne.

SHEIKH ZAYED'S FOREIGN trips, whether of an official business or informal nature, were to carve strong foundations for the future international profile of the UAE. He was known, with remarkable foresight, to embrace the best professional skills from every country that he visited, and then readily implement the same principles, and adapt the methods – from construction to medical practices – to meet the needs of his own country and people. He has won the admiration of many significant world leaders for his tenacity and enterprising projects, attributes that are evident through the continual progress of the Emirates.

An informal photograph of Sheikh Zayed on a safari in the Sudan.

An official visit to France – the UAE's President inspects the welcoming guard of honour in the presence of French President Giscard d'Estaing.

Dr Sheikh Sultan bin Mohammed Al Qassimi, Ruler of Sharjah, receives Indira Gandhi, then Prime Minister of India.

UP UNTIL 1947 and the gaining by India of independence – when the present countries of India and Pakistan were formed – administrative matters in the Trucial States were handled from Bombay. The links between the subcontinent and the UAE that were formed in those times have continued to grow, particularly with Pakistan, with whom the sharing of Islam makes for a common bond.

There were commercial ties too. Much of the pearl trade was handled through dealers in Bombay, who acted as intermediaries between the producers in the Gulf and the buyers in India, Europe and America.

Sheikh Zayed and his entourage at Dubai International Airport.

Sheikh Zayed, leaving for a hunting trip in Pakistan, is seen off by Sheikh Rashid, Political Agent David Roberts, and PIA officials.

Sheikh Zayed, Sultan Qaboos of Oman, Sheikh Mohammed bin Rashid and Sheikh Rashid stand to attention to the guard of honour at Al Ain during his 1973 official visit to the Emirates.

WHILST BAHRAIN AND Qatar had eventually decided to become separate countries, the close contacts that had been established between the states of the Gulf in the period leading up to federation were maintained – and helped, 10 years later, in the formation of the Gulf Co-operation Council, whose members include Kuwait, Bahrain, Saudi Arabia, Qatar and Oman as well as the United Arab Emirates.

Although designed primarily to further peacetime activities the GCC also extends to defence matters – and the unified action of its members in the liberation of Kuwait after the Iraqi invasion proved the soundness of the organisation and the determination of the states of which it is comprised.

Inspecting military manoeuvres, right to left: Crown Prince of Abu Dhabi Sheikh Khalifa, Crown Prince of Bahrain Sheikh Hamad bin Isa, and Head of Abu Dhabi Police Force Sheikh Mubarak bin Mohammed.

Sheikh Rashid, King Faisal of Saudi Arabia and Sheikh Rashid bin Humaid Al Nuaimi, Ruler of Ajman at Dubai's Zabeel Palace.

Queen Elizabeth II of Great Britain was presented with the key of the city by Chairman of Dubai Municipality, Sheikh Hamdan bin Rashid – now also Deputy Ruler, during her visit to the city in 1979. Looking on are Kamal Hamza, Director of Dubai Municipality and Mehdi Al Tajir, UAE Ambassador to the United Kingdom.

THE OLD TIES with Britain have been maintained not only through the large numbers of British expatriates who work in the country – some of whom have been here since long before federation – but by regular visits from members of the British Royal Family, politicians and trade delegations from Chambers of Commerce and Industry associations.

Leading British politicians were – and still are – frequent visitors and their discussions with the Rulers of the Emirates, both before and after federation have covered a wide variety of subjects, ranging from trade to defence. Britain's heir to the throne, Prince Charles, has long maintained a particular interest in furthering the understanding between Muslims and Christians.

Noor Ali Rashid with Edward Heath and Douglas Hurd during their 1968 visit to the UAE.

Visiting Dubai on business, Jeremy Thorpe, former leader of the British Liberal Party, takes time out to stroll by the creek.

UNLIKE THE FREQUENT comings and goings of today, visits by official delegations from overseas were unusual before the late 1960s – and that of the Secretary General of the Arab League caused something of a stir throughout the Trucial States. Now, the UAE is an active participant in the affairs of many international and regional organisations, including the Arab League, Islamic Conference Organisation and OPEC.

Sheikh Ahmed bin Rashid Al Mualla, Ruler of Umm Al Quwain being gently jostled by the enthusiastic crowds, awaits the arrival of Abdul Khaliq Hassouna, Secretary General of the Arab League.

A motorcade taking delegates of the Arab League from Dubai to Sharjah attracted a popular following. It must have been a dusty progress before the opening of the surfaced road linking the two emirates.

A festival in Fujairah to welcome the Secretary General of the Arab League.

The 1964 visit of the Arab League Delegation brought political and social awareness to the area when Egyptian leader Gamal Abdul Nasser's popularity was widespread.

THE ARAB LEAGUE was founded in Cairo in 1945 to promote Arab unity, its initial members being Egypt, Syria, Iraq, Lebanon, Jordan, Saudi Arabia and Yemen. Egypt was to play an important role in the development of the region, supplying many teachers, doctors, engineers, administrators and other professionals to various Arab nations, including the Trucial States.

The Egyptian leader, Gamal Abdul Nasser, was held in very high regard by the people of the UAE, and in Dubai one of the city's squares was named after him. On his death in 1970 huge crowds spontaneously assembled in the towns and cities of the country to mourn his passing.

A procession at Khor Fakkan: the crowd bears portraits of Arab leader Gamal Abdul Nasser.

Noor Ali accompanied Arab League Secretary General Abdul Khaliq Hassouna and delegation members throughout their visits to each of the emirates.

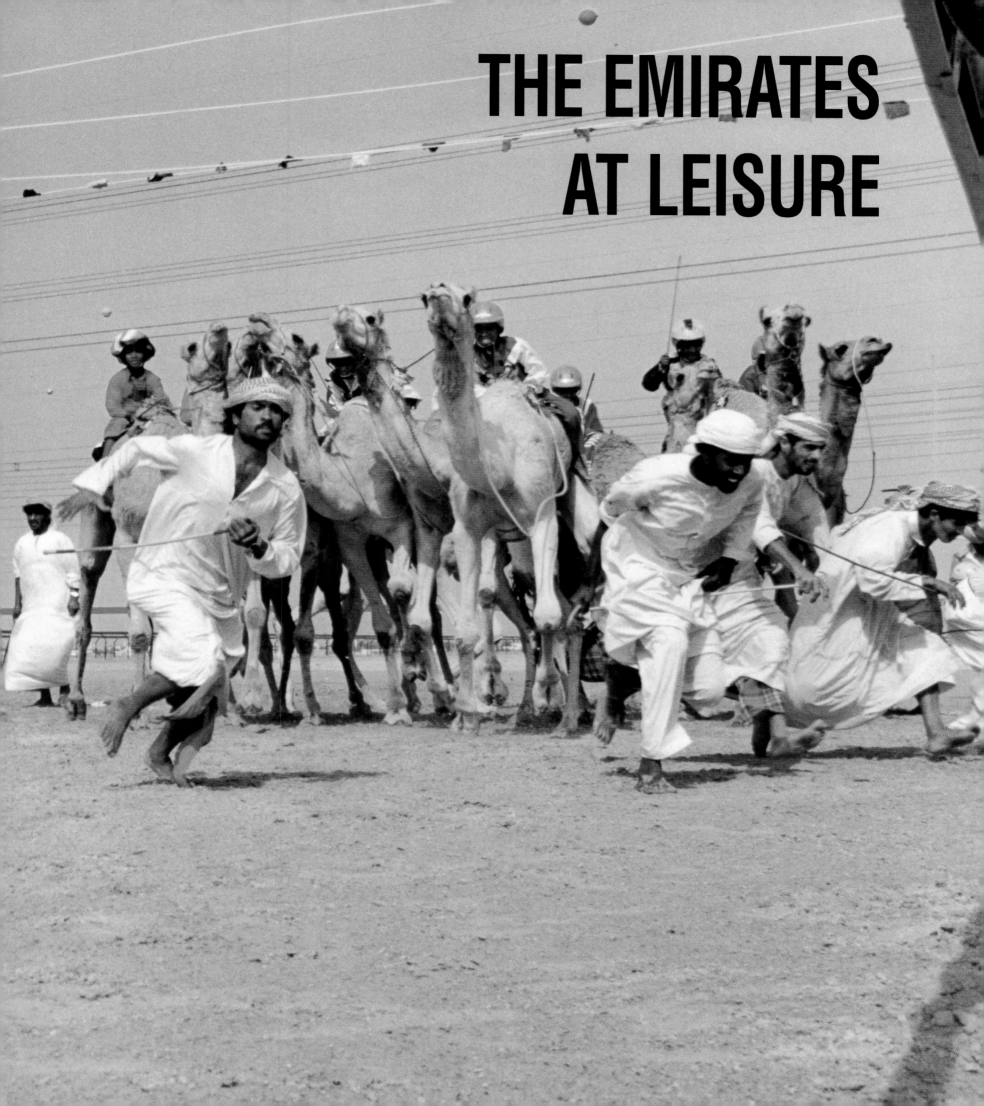

THE EMIRATES
AT LEISURE

Across the creek from the Political Agency a large crowd has gathered to celebrate the visit of a foreign dignitary. Noor Ali's picture, taken from where Dubai Municipality now stands, has something of the flavour of a L S Lowry painting.

Previous pages: The start of a
camel race. A centuries-old
scene updated only by the power
cables, starting tapes and
riders' helmets.

EIDS, WEDDINGS AND other festive occasions were often celebrated at open-air gatherings at which traditional dances and songs were performed. Some of the more popular folk dances were the *naiashti*, in which colourfully dressed ladies swing their long hair in time to sweeping rhythms of drums and, sometimes, pipes; the *ardha*, a dance for men, to the beat of a tambourine-like drum; and the *razfa*, a complex routine in which two groups, singing alternate lines of tribal folk songs, weave back and forth. Songs and dances draw not only on traditional Arabic themes, but have also absorbed Nubian and East African influences – areas with which the people of the Emirates have had long trading links. The Arab love of poetry and word-play featured strongly in the songs.

To the accompaniment of drums and the occasional feu de joie a traditional dance takes place – although participants were now arriving by car rather than camel.

Adopting the traditional stance during a popular folk dance, this youth takes centre stage with great solemnity.

A small celebration at Ras Al Khaimah in the early 60s.

CLASSICAL LOCAL INSTRUMENTS reflect the limited materials available for their construction in years gone by. Drums were made from animal skins stretched tightly over wooden frames and kept taut by warming them over braziers of hot charcoal, bagpipes were made from the stomach of a goat, and the *tamboura* – a stringed instrument somewhat like a harp but with a sound-box similar to that of a guitar – was of wood and skin. Even goats' hooves were put to good use: they were stitched on to a length of cloth which was then wrapped around the waist of the dancer whose movements made them clack and clatter like multiple castanets.

Drums were not always made of traditional materials – as with much folk music around the world any handy item could be pressed into service.

WEDDINGS ARE THE occasions for some of the most joyous and colourful celebrations of all. The bride's house is often decorated with festoons of thousands of lights, feasts are held and the festivities can continue for several days. For members of prominent families the celebrations can extend way beyond family and friends – public entertainment frequently being arranged, including camel races, dances and musical performances to which all are invited.

These young ladies display fine henna designs on their hands as well as ornate jewellery in styles typical of the region.

In all their regalia, the women contributed a colourful and decorative charm in the ceremonial ritual of weddings.

All dressed up for Eid.

Nowadays more formal racetracks provide the venue for meetings but not so long ago races were held on any convenient bit of desert with firm sand. The Maktoums are keen horsemen, as evidenced here by Sheikh Mohammed bin Rashid.

LOCAL SPORTS – PARTICULARLY camel and horse-racing – not only offer the excitement of the events themselves but also the opportunity to maintain traditions that might otherwise be lost.

Camel-racing grew out of the need to improve the breeding and physical characteristics of a beast upon which the inhabitants relied extensively for transport in the days before the four-wheel drive took over as the main means of getting about in the desert. Nowadays many are bred exclusively for racing and good examples are worth millions of dirhams. The races can be over distances as long as 16 kilometres, providing a gruelling test of stamina. Whilst the working camel had to survive for long periods without water and would have had to eat whatever was available, latter-day racing animals are pampered by highly-skilled keepers who monitor a strict regime of diet and exercise.

The oil-drums that used to mark camel-race tracks have now been replaced by specially built fencing.

Overleaf: Jostling camel jockeys make a frenzied spurt along the final furlong to the finish.

A display of traditional sailing skills during a heritage festival in Dubai.

THE FORTUNES OF a people who for generations made much of their livelihood from the sea depended heavily on the quality of their boats and the skills of their seamen, whether for trading, fishing or pearling. Whilst the craft of the shipwright and the competence of crews are no longer of such vital economic importance, the traditional expertise is still demonstrated in races featuring both rowing and sailing boats.

Rowing boat races – involving boats of 20 metres and more in length propelled by upwards of 100 oarsmen – are fiercely contested, the honour of each emirate relying on the muscle-power of the crews. The racing dhows or *jalboots*, from which the naval term jollyboat is derived, are not merely symbols of a bygone age: the fishermen of the UAE still put out to reap the rich harvest of the Gulf waters.

A demonstration of more modern forms of aquatic skills – Sheikh Ahmed bin Rashid on the skis and Sheikh Butti on the boat.

**Sheikh Mohammed bin Rashid
with an Egyptian Shooting Team
at the conclusion of a contest
held at Manama, Ajman.**

**Sheikh Rashid's falconer at the
Ruler's Office overlooking
the creek.**

IN RECENT YEARS traditional sports have been supplemented by others brought in from different parts of the world. Just a generation or so ago football matches were played on any flat piece of desert; now modern stadia provide superb venues for the game – and the UAE team even made it into the 1990 World Cup finals. Up until less than a decade ago golfers would play on to browns (areas of sand tamped down with oil) instead of greens and carry a piece of astroturf around with them for use as a tee; now Dubai offers a choice of three championship grass courses. Dhow-racing is supplemented by power-boats and pearl-diving by scuba-diving.

Throughout the country, whilst the youth have been encouraged to maintain an interest in the traditional sports, other activities have also received official support and the fixtures list boasts some of the top international names in most major sports.

Football has become the national game of the UAE and there is intense rivalry between clubs.

Noor Ali, centre, with the first cricket team to visit the UAE, which comprised many of the Pakistan national team's stars.

A bicycle race forms part of the
Sports Day events at a
Sharjah school.

The first school for girls opened
in Sharjah in 1954. Now there are
some 550 government schools
and nearly 300 private schools
in the country.

FEW CHANGES THAT have been wrought in the country have had greater effect than the provision of universal education. In 1971 there were less than 44,000 pupils in schools; there are now over 450,000 and schools may be found not only in the cities but throughout the country in high mountain villages and tiny settlements in the desert. Additionally, there are some 15,000 students undertaking further education at the Higher Colleges of Technology and Emirates University at Al Ain. The new generations, which Sheikh Zayed refers to as the real wealth of the nation, have access to opportunities unknown to their fathers and mothers.

For the first time in the history of the Emirates, girl students of Sharjah were seen participating in parades on the occasion of the 1964 visit of the Arab league delegation.

Sheikh Nahyan bin Mubarak, now Minister of Higher Education and Scientific Research, has made a major contribution to preparing the younger generations to assume a key role in the country's economy.

135

Scouts parade through Dubai in 1963. The display was in support of Arab unity at a time when Egypt was attempting to form the United Arab Republic – a federation of Egypt, Syria and Iraq. Although Egypt retained the title of UAR until 1971 the proposed union never fully developed.

Scouts at Umm Al Quwain.

BEFORE THE ARRIVAL of sophisticated sports facilities, television and video games, there were the simpler pleasures of scouting – still popular amongst young men and women in the UAE. Founded by Robert Baden-Powell in 1908, the Scout Association was designed to inculcate the concept and practice of good citizenship whilst instilling in the young a sense of competition and personal discipline.

Sheikh Khalifa bin Saeed Al Maktoum, brother of Sheikh Rashid, poses casually with, from left, Sheikh Ahmed bin Maktoum, Sheikh Hasher bin Maktoum, Sheikh Mana bin Khalifa and Sheikh Butti bin Maktoum.

Sheikh Ahmed bin Rashid Al Mualla of Umm Al Quwain proudly posing with his grandsons.

An early meeting of the Ladies' Association in Dubai, whose founder members included Mrs Tullock (first from left, second row), Mrs Chapman (second from right, second row), and Mrs Jashanmal (second from right, front row). Donald Hawley looks suitably pleased to be surrounded by such a charming and distinguished group.

Party time at Dubai's Al Bustan Hotel – complete with silly hats. Some national celebrations are more embarrassing than others!

EXPATRIATE GAMES. THE variety of nationalities living and working in the UAE brought their own customs, pastimes and cuisine. In turn, the tolerance displayed by the people of the UAE to the differing habits of foreigners has enriched the social and cultural life of the country.

As the country has grown so too has the number of nationalities who reside here. From Asia and the Americas, Europe, Africa and Australia they have come, to do business in one of the fastest developing nations in the world. But, whilst the range of cultures is immense – there can be few more cosmopolitan places on the planet than the major cities of the UAE – the Arab traditions have not been lost and still form, through religion, social conventions and a common heritage, the bedrock of society.

Sheikh Ahmed bin Hamed, the former Minister of Information and Culture, at the inauguration of Abu Dhabi's Indian Unity Club. The club developed over the years into the Indian Sports Club, before adopting its current title of the Indian Social Centre. Seated next to him is Mr Bojraj, from one of the oldest Indian trading families to have settled in Abu Dhabi.

Children, including those of Political Agent James Craig and his wife, sit with Sharjah Ruler Sheikh Saqr bin Sultan during Eid of 1962. Sharjah was renowned for its contribution towards these special occasions.